FOOTBALL
All-Stars

Celebrate greatness on the field

Kane Miller
A DIVISION OF EDC PUBLISHING

First American Edition 2020
Kane Miller, A Division of EDC Publishing

For information contact
Kane Miller, A Division of EDC Publishing
5402 S 122nd E Ave
Tulsa, OK 74146
www.kanemiller.com
www.edcpub.com
www.usbornebooksandmore.com

ISBN 978-1-68464-137-6
Library of Congress Control Number: 2019952934

Printed in China, January 2021.

Image credits A.J. Green © Frank Victores/AP/Shutterstock, Aaron Donald © Kyusung Gong/AP/Shutterstock, Aaron
Rodgers © Adam Hunger/AP/Shutterstock, Barry Sanders © Jerry Coli/Dreamstime.com, Bobby Wagner © Chris Szagola/CSM/
Shutterstock, C.J. Mosley © Bill Kostroun/AP/Shutterstock, Calais Campbell © Stephen B Morton/AP/Shutterstock, Cam
Newton © Elise Amendola/AP/Shutterstock, Cameron Wake © Phelan Ebenhack/ AP/Shutterstock, Christian McCaffrey
© Walter Arce/Dreamstime.com, Clay Matthews © Rick Scuteri/AP/ Shutterstock, Darius Leonard © Mark LoMoglio/AP/
Shutterstock, David Bakhtiari © Duane Burleson/AP/Shutterstock, DeAndre Hopkins © Reed Hoffmann/AP/ Shutterstock,
Derwin James © Phelan M Ebenhack/AP/Shutterstock, Dick Butkus © Jerry Coli/Dreamstime.com, Drew Brees © Jonathan
Mailhes/CSM/Shutterstock, Earl Thomas © Nick Wass/AP/Shutterstock, Eric Berry © Reed Hoffmann/AP/Shutterstock, Geno
Atkins © David Richard/AP/Shutterstock, George Kittle © Gregory Payan/AP/ Shutterstock, Gerald McCoy © Mike McCarn/AP/
Shutterstock, J. J. Watt © Eric Christian Smith/AP/ Shutterstock, Jerry Rice © Jerry Coli/Dreamstime.com, Joe Greene © Jerry
Coli/Dreamstime.com, Joe Montana © Jerry Coli/Dreamstime.com, Johnny Unitas © Commons.wikimedia.org/The Sporting
News archives/Public Domain, JuJu Smith-Schuster © Gene Puskar/AP/Shutterstock, Julio Jones © John Bazemore/AP/
Shutterstock, Justin Houston © Phelan M Ebenhack/AP/Shutterstock, Khalil Mack © Brad Penner/AP/Shutterstock, Kirk
Cousins © Tony Avelar/AP/Shutterstock, Lavonte David © Jason Behnken/ AP/Shutterstock, Le'Veon Bell © Jeff Haynes/AP/
Shutterstock, Leighton Vander Esch © Jeff Haynes/AP/ Shutterstock, Luke Kuechly © John Bazemore/AP/Shutterstock, Marshal
Yanda © Ron Schwane/AP/Shutterstock, Matt Ryan © Commons.wikimedia.org/Keith Allison, Michael Bennett © Jeff Haynes/
AP/Shutterstock, Michael Thomas © Jonathan Mailhes/CSM/Shutterstock, Mike Evans © Phelan M Ebenhack/AP/Shutterstock,
Ndamukong Suh © Jeff Haynes/AP/Shutterstock, Patrick Mahomes © Elise Amendola/AP/Shutterstock, Philip Rivers © Marcio
Jose Sanchez/AP/Shutterstock, Reggie White © Jerry Coli/ Dreamstime.com, Richard Sherman © Marcio Jose Sanchez/AP/
Shutterstock, Ronnie Lott © Jerry Coli/Dreamstime.com, Russell Wilson © Larry Maurer/Commons.wikimedia.org, Sam
Bradford © Ralph Freso/AP/Shutterstock, Saquon Barkley © KA Sports Photos/flickr.com, Stephon Gilmore © Winslow
Townson/AP/Shutterstock, Todd Gurley © Commons.wikimedia.org/Mario957, Tom Brady © Dave Shopland/BPI/Shutterstock,
Tony Gonzalez © Jerry Coli/Dreamstime.com, Tre'Davious White © Adrian Kraus/AP/Shutterstock, Trent Williams © Rick
Scuteri/ AP/Shutterstock, Tyron Smith © Tony Gutierrez/AP/Shutterstock, Von Miller © Jack Dempsey/AP/Shutterstock,
Walter Payton © Jerry Coli/Dreamstime.com, Zack Martin © Commons.wikimedia.org Keith Allison/Public Domain.

CONTENTS

TOP 10 ALL-TIME LEGENDS

Players who stand head and shoulders above the rest in football's pantheon of greats.

1 JERRY RICE

 1985–2005   2010

For 20 seasons, "Flash 80" would catch any pass near him and carve routes through the defense. In 2020, Rice still holds over 100 NFL records, some beating the runner-up by 50 percent. He was not the biggest, strongest, or fastest, but through relentless training and dedication, Rice dominated.

WIDE RECEIVER

2 BARRY SANDERS

 1989–1998 1989–1998 2004

Sanders' 40-yard time was 4.37 seconds. He could start, turn, and reverse on a dime. Tackles simply missed him. One coach had his defensive linemen chase chickens because it mimicked this RB's elusiveness. Sanders created holes, went around defenses, and his rushing yards record still stands.

RUNNING BACK

3 WALTER PAYTON

 1975–1987 1993

Payton's nickname "Sweetness" refers to his personality and athletic elegance, and pokes fun at his all-out "never die easy" approach to the game. He ranks second in NFL career rushing yards and his eight touchdown passes remain an RB record. Payton's unique "stutter-step" maneuver put opponents on the back foot.

RUNNING BACK

4 JOE MONTANA

 1979–1994   2000

"Joe Cool" was known for his calmness in the middle of chaos, especially with the game on the line in the 4th quarter. Montana's quick reads, signal calls, and timing helped his team come from behind in 31 games. Montana led his team to four Super Bowls and was named MVP in three of them.

QUARTERBACK

JERRY RICE

RECORD BREAKER

He finished his career with a stellar 22,895 receiving yards in 303 games. He missed only 17 games over 20 NFL regular seasons.

5 REGGIE WHITE

 1984–2000 2006

White's six feet five inches and 300 pounds barreled through blockers like they were "on roller skates." The "Minister of Defense" – he was an ordained minister – retains the NFL record for nine straight seasons with 10-plus sacks. This bigger-than-life pass rusher was the real deal.

DEFENSIVE END

These players may no longer be in the game, but their achievements are pressed into the turf and burned into history. Their big plays, record-setting games, and unique antics are the stuff of legend among fans. Current players are honored when compared to one of these giants. Which one is your choice for best of the best?

6 TONY GONZALEZ

 1997–2013 2019

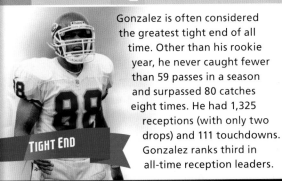

Gonzalez is often considered the greatest tight end of all time. Other than his rookie year, he never caught fewer than 59 passes in a season and surpassed 80 catches eight times. He had 1,325 receptions (with only two drops) and 111 touchdowns. Gonzalez ranks third in all-time reception leaders.

TIGHT END

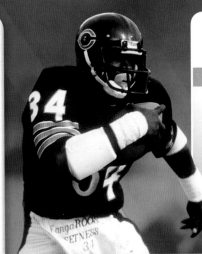

WALTER PAYTON
RUSHING LEGEND

In 1977, with the Chicago Bears facing the Minnesota Vikings, Walter rushed for 275 yards on 40 carries. This NFL record stood until 2000.

7 JOHNNY UNITAS

 1955–1973 1979

Originally signed as a backup for the Colts, Unitas went on to change the game of football with his confidence, leadership, play-calling genius, and passing skill. His record of 47 consecutive games with a touchdown stood for 52 years. "The Golden Arm" was named NFL Player of the Year three times and named to 10 Pro Bowls.

QUARTERBACK

8 DICK BUTKUS

1965–1973 1979

In high school, Butkus worked out by pushing a car up and down the street outside his home. On the field, he crushed opponents. "The Enforcer" was feared and intimidating. He ripped the ball from carriers' hands, amassing 22 interceptions and recovering 27 opponent fumbles.

MIDDLE LINEBACKER

9 JOE GREENE

 1969–1981 1987

Even in the era of the "Steel Curtain" defense, Greene dominated. He had size, speed, and instincts. Greene took down opposing linemen with ease. Described as "mobile and hostile," he recorded an interception, forced fumble, and fumble recovery in the 1975 Super Bowl.

DEFENSIVE TACKLE

10 RONNIE LOTT

1981–1995 2000

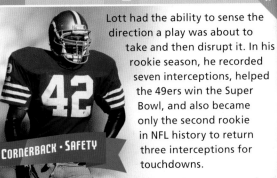

Lott had the ability to sense the direction a play was about to take and then disrupt it. In his rookie season, he recorded seven interceptions, helped the 49ers win the Super Bowl, and also became only the second rookie in NFL history to return three interceptions for touchdowns.

CORNERBACK · SAFETY

All-Stars
Hall of Fame

Fifty first-class players with Hall of Fame potential:

AARON DONALD 1 — Defensive Tackle	**DREW BREES** 2 — Quarterback	**KHALIL MACK** 3 — Outside Linebacker	**PATRICK MAHOMES** 4 — Quarterback	**TODD GURLEY** 5 — Running Back
TOM BRADY 6 — Quarterback	**AARON RODGERS** 7 — Quarterback	**JULIO JONES** 8 — Wide Receiver	**VON MILLER** 9 — Outside Linebacker	**DEANDRE HOPKINS** 10 — Wide Receiver
J. J. WATT 11 — Defensive End	**MICHAEL THOMAS** 12 — Wide Receiver	**BOBBY WAGNER** 13 — Middle Linebacker	**SAQUON BARKLEY** 14 — Running Back	**PHILIP RIVERS** 15 — Quarterback
LUKE KUECHLY 16 — Middle Linebacker	**RUSSELL WILSON** 17 — Quarterback	**DARIUS LEONARD** 18 — Outside Linebacker	**GEORGE KITTLE** 19 — Tight End	**DERWIN JAMES** 20 — Free Safety
DAVID BAKHTIARI 21 — Offensive Tackle	**JUJU SMITH-SCHUSTER** 22 — Wide Receiver	**STEPHON GILMORE** 23 — Cornerback	**TYRON SMITH** 24 — Offensive Tackle	**MIKE EVANS** 25 — Wide Receiver

These are players with exceptional talent and drive. They outwork, out hustle, outplay, and out win the competition, leaving nothing on the field except glory and inspirational moments. Imagine the team you could put together if you had your pick of these players! Who would make the final cut?

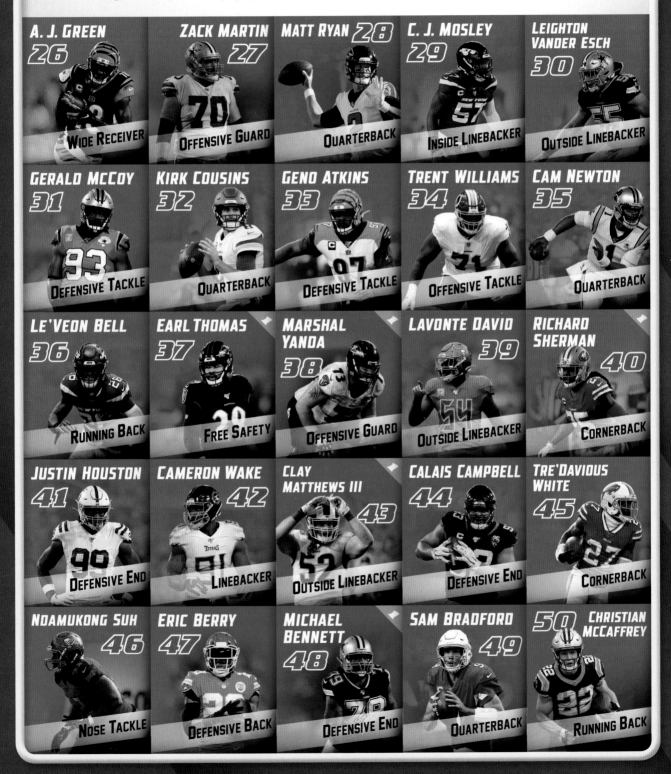

A. J. GREEN 26	ZACK MARTIN 27	MATT RYAN 28	C. J. MOSLEY 29	LEIGHTON VANDER ESCH 30
WIDE RECEIVER	OFFENSIVE GUARD	QUARTERBACK	INSIDE LINEBACKER	OUTSIDE LINEBACKER
GERALD MCCOY 31	KIRK COUSINS 32	GENO ATKINS 33	TRENT WILLIAMS 34	CAM NEWTON 35
DEFENSIVE TACKLE	QUARTERBACK	DEFENSIVE TACKLE	OFFENSIVE TACKLE	QUARTERBACK
LE'VEON BELL 36	EARL THOMAS 37	MARSHAL YANDA 38	LAVONTE DAVID 39	RICHARD SHERMAN 40
RUNNING BACK	FREE SAFETY	OFFENSIVE GUARD	OUTSIDE LINEBACKER	CORNERBACK
JUSTIN HOUSTON 41	CAMERON WAKE 42	CLAY MATTHEWS III 43	CALAIS CAMPBELL 44	TRE'DAVIOUS WHITE 45
DEFENSIVE END	LINEBACKER	OUTSIDE LINEBACKER	DEFENSIVE END	CORNERBACK
NDAMUKONG SUH 46	ERIC BERRY 47	MICHAEL BENNETT 48	SAM BRADFORD 49	CHRISTIAN MCCAFFREY 50
NOSE TACKLE	DEFENSIVE BACK	DEFENSIVE END	QUARTERBACK	RUNNING BACK

AARON DONALD — Page 10

MARSHAL YANDA — Page 28

MICHAEL THOMAS — Page 19

AARON RODGERS — Page 14

LUKE KUECHLY — Page 22

All-Stars
Hall of Fame

STAR PLAYER PROFILES

BOBBY WAGNER — Page 20

VON MILLER — Page 16

TYRON SMITH — Page 24

TOM BRADY — Page 13

LE'VEON BELL — Page 27

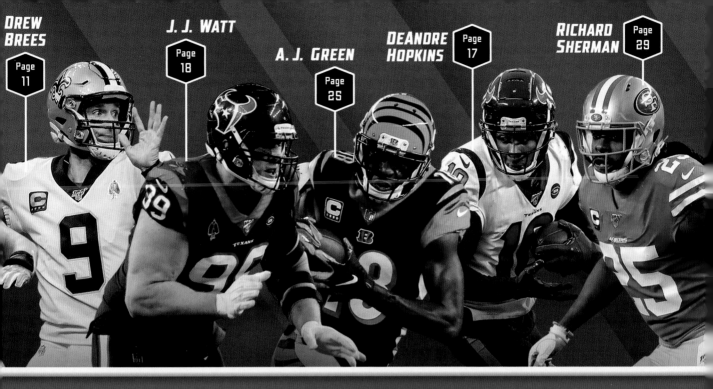

Discover more about the person behind the face mask, and the athlete under the shoulder pads: these top 20 players are the elite of the elite, but what gives the Tom Bradys, Drew Breeses, Aaron Donalds, and Khalil Macks their edge?

Read on to find out.

AARON DONALD

All-Stars
Hall of Fame
1

His nickname is "Cheat Code"—he does whatever it takes.

The awards keep coming for Aaron, one of the greatest interior defensive linemen of all time. He deserves the honors—and the stellar $135 million contract. From the age of 12, his father worked with this one-man wrecking crew on strength, speed, and agility. Aaron can mow down a QB and RB at the same time! Sacks per season record is 22.5—Aaron's at 20.5!

PERSONAL DATA

 May 23, 1991

 Pittsburgh, Pennsylvania

 6 ft. 1 in.

 280 lb.

CAREER HISTORY

ST. LOUIS / LOS ANGELES RAMS

2014 –

☆ 99 ☆

CAREER HIGHLIGHTS

- Six consecutive Pro Bowl and five first team All-Pro selections.
- Two-time NFL Defensive Player of the Year, and ranked No.1 in NFL Top 100.
- Led the league in regular season with TFL 25 (2018) and 20 (2019).

OFFENSIVE TACKLE

☆ ☆ ☆

DREW BREES

All-Stars
Hall of Fame
2

He's the comeback king with a golden arm that can do no wrong.

Saints fans know him as "Breesus." He helped New Orleans heal after Hurricane Katrina, and blessed the city with its only Super Bowl win in 2009. As QBs go, Drew is a legend. His passing skills are amazing, and he set an all-time, single-game record in 2019 with a 96.7 completion percentage—30 passes, 29 completed! In 2013, he joined the 50,000-yard club in record time.

PERSONAL DATA

📅 January 15, 1979

📍 Dallas, Texas

⬆ 6 ft. 0 in.

⚖ 209 lb.

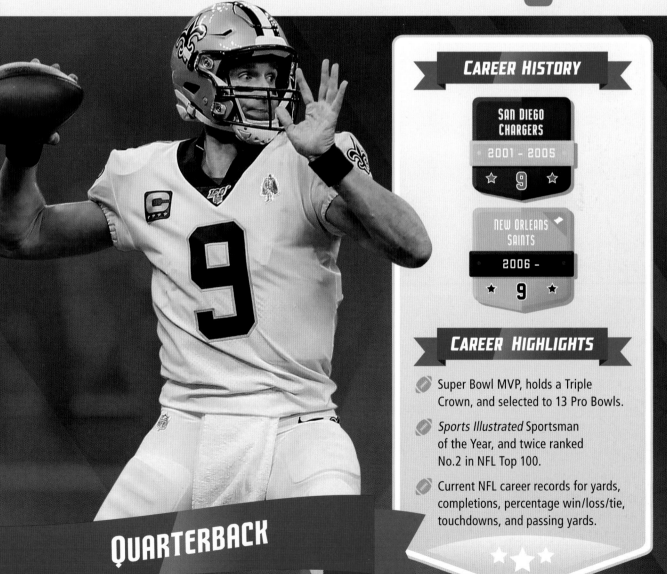

CAREER HISTORY

SAN DIEGO CHARGERS
2001 - 2005
★ 9 ★

NEW ORLEANS SAINTS
2006 -
★ 9 ★

CAREER HIGHLIGHTS

🏈 Super Bowl MVP, holds a Triple Crown, and selected to 13 Pro Bowls.

🏈 *Sports Illustrated* Sportsman of the Year, and twice ranked No.2 in NFL Top 100.

🏈 Current NFL career records for yards, completions, percentage win/loss/tie, touchdowns, and passing yards.

QUARTERBACK

KHALIL MACK

All-Stars
Hall of Fame
3

Khalil sets a goal, maps a path to it, and sticks to it 110 percent.

His $141 million Bears contract is currently the highest ever for a non-QB, but this quiet defender lets his pass rushing do all the talking. By age seven, Khalil could do 60 military style push-ups. He wore number 46 in college—his *EA Sports* potential rating out of 99—to motivate himself to improve. He succeeded by a long way: Khalil dominates destructive defense in the NFL.

PERSONAL DATA

February 22, 1991

Fort Pierce, Florida

6 ft. 3 in.

269 lb.

CAREER HISTORY

OAKLAND RAIDERS
2014 – 2017
★ 52 ★

CHICAGO BEARS
2018 –
★ 52 ★

CAREER HIGHLIGHTS

- First in NFL history selected first team All-Pro in two positions in one season.
- Five Pro Bowl and three first team All-Pro selections.
- Two-time pro winner Butkus Award, and NFL and MAC Defensive Player of the Year.

OUTSIDE LINEBACKER

TOM BRADY

All-Stars
Hall of Fame
6

"Tom Terrific"—the best draft ever made by the Patriots.

You just can't beat the records Tom's set and the awards he's received. The oldest QB in the current NFL is surely G.O.A.T. material. His natural ability, hard work, and intelligence combine with a sixth sense about the passing pocket. Tom led the Patriots to more division titles than any QB, including a perfect 16–0 regular season in 2007. This QB is today's benchmark for greatness.

PERSONAL DATA

August 3, 1977

San Mateo, California

6 ft. 4 in.

225 lb.

CAREER HISTORY

NEW ENGLAND PATRIOTS
2000 – 2019
★ 12 ★

TAMPA BAY BUCCANEERS
2020 –
★ 12 ★

CAREER HIGHLIGHTS

- Record-setting 20 seasons, nine Super Bowl appearances, and six Lombardi Trophies with one team.

- Currently tops all QBs in total season wins (219), career passing yards, and touchdowns.

- Three-time NFL MVP, Athlete of the Decade, and 14 Pro Bowl selections.

QUARTERBACK

AARON RODGERS

All-Stars
Hall of Fame
7

He is one of the most lethal and accurate deep-ball passers in the game.

As a two-year-old, Aaron would watch NFL games silently. Three years later, he was naming formations and throwing a football through a tire ring. He is strong armed, fast, and has a core of iron. Aaron's 2011 over 400 passing yards with four touchdowns in a single game was so magical, he did it again in 2018! His secret is visualizing the win before the game and then making it real.

PERSONAL DATA

December 2, 1983

Chico, California

6 ft. 2 in.

225 lb.

CAREER HISTORY

GREEN BAY PACKERS

2005 –

12

CAREER HIGHLIGHTS

- Current NFL record for 402 consecutive passes without interception.

- Two-time NFL MVP, a Super Bowl MVP, and *Associated Press* Athlete of the Year.

- Eight Pro Bowl and two All-Pro selections.

QUARTERBACK

JULIO JONES

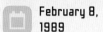

All-Stars Hall of Fame 8

He has it all—speed, intelligence, athleticism, and team spirit.

Julio was a five-star high school athlete, and his athleticism shows on the field. His 4.39-second 40-yard dash is only part of the package—there's also his leaping, body control, and ace catching. In 2019, Julio became the quickest (in just 125 NFL games) to amass 12,000 career passing yards. The Falcons lost the Super Bowl in 2016, but there's plenty more to come from this elite wide receiver.

PERSONAL DATA

February 8, 1989

Foley, Alabama

6 ft. 3 in.

220 lb.

CAREER HISTORY

ATLANTA FALCONS

2011 –

★ 11 ★

CAREER HIGHLIGHTS

- Seven Pro Bowl and two All-Pro selections.
- Only player in NFL history to have a five-week streak of more than 1,400 yards receiving.
- Current NFL record for receiving yards per game (96.2, beating the record by 8.7 yards).

WIDE RECEIVER

VON MILLER

All-Stars
Hall of Fame
9

He wears 58 to honor Pro Footballer Hall of Fame linebacker Derrick Thomas.

Von's record contract for a defensive player lets him do more of the things he loves: dancing, raising chickens, and promoting his children's charity. This four-star high school athlete with All-American honors, Butkus Awards, and near-perfect size, speed (4.49-second 40-yard dash), and agility, was destined for greatness. He proved it in Super Bowl 50 with 2.5 sacks.

PERSONAL DATA

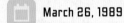

March 26, 1989

Dallas, Texas

6 ft. 3 in.

250 lb.

CAREER HISTORY

DENVER BRONCOS

2011 –

★ 58 ★

CAREER HIGHLIGHTS

- Eight Pro Bowl and seven All-Pro selections.
- NFL Defensive Rookie of the Year and Super Bowl MVP.
- Ranked No.2 in NFL Top 100 (2017).

OUTSIDE LINEBACKER

DeAndre Hopkins

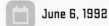

All-Stars
Hall of Fame
10

He's not the biggest or the fastest, but covering DeAndre can be the hardest.

In 2018, this wide receiver had 115 catches and zero drops. How does he do it? DeAndre's hands are huge—10 inches from little finger to thumb—and very strong. He uses a gripper to exercise his hands and fingers, and his size XXXXL gloves at the end of his ultra-long arms give him a huge advantage. With catlike agility, he can reach the impossible pass and defy cover.

PERSONAL DATA

- June 6, 1992
- Central, South Carolina
- 6 ft. 1 in.
- 212 lb.

CAREER HISTORY

HOUSTON TEXANS
2013 – 2019
★ 10 ★

ARIZONA CARDINALS
2020 –
★ 10 ★

CAREER HIGHLIGHTS

- Pro Football Writers Association (PFWA) All-Rookie team selection.
- Four Pro Bowl and three first team All-Pro selections.
- NFL receiving touchdowns leader (2017).

WIDE RECEIVER

J. J. WATT

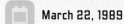
Even on vacation, J.J. starts his workout at 3:45 a.m.

His opponents say his game is almost flawless. Scouts praise his athleticism, strength, and versatility. In 2014, he broke a 70-year drought for a defensive lineman scoring five touchdowns in a season. J.J. was the first in NFL history to record two 20-plus season sacks in a career. And according to J.J., the best is yet to come. Expect more impact plays, one-handed sacks, and plays against the run.

PERSONAL DATA

March 22, 1989

Waukesha, Wisconsin

6 ft. 5 in.

288 lb.

CAREER HISTORY

HOUSTON TEXANS

2011 –

☆ **99** ☆

CAREER HIGHLIGHTS

- Five Pro Bowl and five All-Pro selections.

- Walter Payton NFL Man of the Year and *Sports Illustrated* Sportsman of the Year.

- Three-time NFL Defensive Player of the Year, and ranked No.1 on NFL Top 100 (2015).

★ ★ ★

DEFENSIVE END

MICHAEL THOMAS

All-Stars
Hall of Fame
12

"Can't Guard Mike" is on his way to wide receiver legend status.

In junior high, Michael's teammates laughed when he said he would play football like his uncle, Keyshawn Johnson. Those guys aren't laughing now. Michael is the most productive pass catcher in the game. He always finds a way to get into the open. In common with DeAndre Hopkins, there's always a hand exerciser within his reach. He only has one speed—fast—and if you're in front of him, you are in his way!

PERSONAL DATA

📅 March 3, 1993

📍 Los Angeles, California

⬆ 6 ft. 3 in.

💼 212 lb.

CAREER HISTORY

NEW ORLEANS SAINTS

2016 –

☆　13　☆

CAREER HIGHLIGHTS

 NFL OPOY (2019) and current NFL record for most receptions in a single season.

🏈 Two Pro Bowl and two first team All-Pro selections.

 More than eight receptions and 85 yards in eight straight games—a first in NFL history.

★ ★ ★

WIDE RECEIVER

BOBBY WAGNER

All-Stars
Hall of Fame
13

A tenacious, silent assassin, who pulls in and wraps up ball carriers.

At Utah State's pro day combine drills in 2012, Bobby floored the scouts with his 40-yard dash, broad jump, and vertical jump. His ability to impress continues. Bobby reads the opposing defenses and is rock solid on tackles, rarely ever missing. In 2019, he broke the Seahawks' all-time tackles record with 989 in just eight seasons. Bobby has been described as being "on the Mount Rushmore of stars."

PERSONAL DATA

June 27, 1990

Los Angeles, California

6 ft. 0 in.

242 lb.

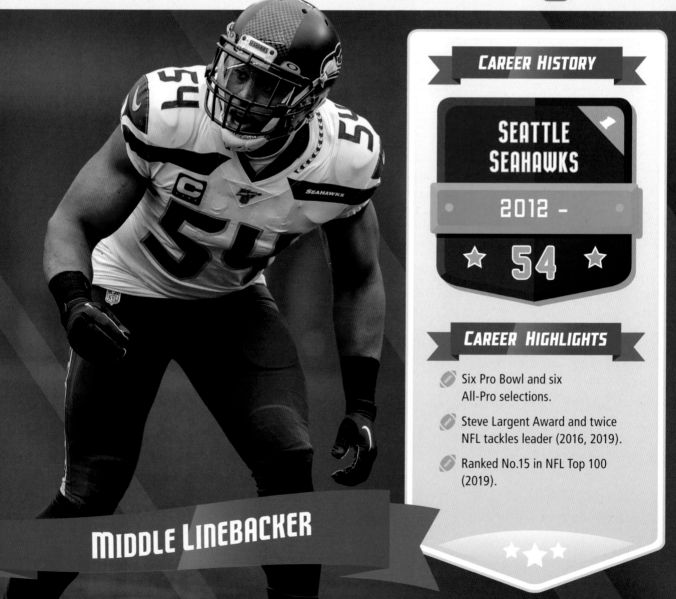

CAREER HISTORY

SEATTLE SEAHAWKS

2012 –

★ 54 ★

CAREER HIGHLIGHTS

- Six Pro Bowl and six All-Pro selections.
- Steve Largent Award and twice NFL tackles leader (2016, 2019).
- Ranked No.15 in NFL Top 100 (2019).

MIDDLE LINEBACKER

★ ★ ★

PHILIP RIVERS

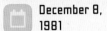

The best QB never to have played or won a Super Bowl.

Philip knew from fifth grade that he was going to play football, and started wearing 17—his father's old number—in ninth grade. He has rewritten the Chargers' passer records and sits sixth on NFL career records for passing yards. Philip is one of the ten QBs in the Pro Football 50,000-yard club. "El Capitan" so loves the game he once played a whole game with a torn knee ligament!

PERSONAL DATA

December 8, 1981

Decatur, Alabama

6 ft. 5 in.

228 lb.

CAREER HISTORY

SAN DIEGO / LOS ANGELES CHARGERS
2004 – 2019
★ 17 ★

INDIANAPOLIS COLTS
2020 –
★ 17 ★

CAREER HIGHLIGHTS

- Eight Pro Bowl selections.
- NFL Comeback Player of the Year (2013).
- Second in all-time consecutive QB starts.

QUARTERBACK

LUKE KUECHLY

All-Stars
Hall of Fame
16

He could read the opponent's next play at the line of scrimmage.

This dominant defender and pass rusher extraordinaire lived up to his "Captain America" nickname. Among his early accolades were All-American twice, Defensive Rookie of the Year, and youngest-ever Defensive Player of the Year. In 2019, after 107 games, he reached 1,000 career tackles! When he retired in January 2020, the only thing missing was a Super Bowl ring.

PERSONAL DATA

 April 20, 1991

 Cincinnati, Ohio

6 ft. 3 in.

238 lb.

CAREER HISTORY

CAROLINA PANTHERS

2012 – 2019

☆ **59** ☆

CAREER HIGHLIGHTS

 Seven Pro Bowl and five first team All-Pro selections.

 Four-time winner Butkus Award (college and pro).

Ranked in NFL Top 100 every year since 2013.

MIDDLE LINEBACKER

DAVID BAKHTIARI

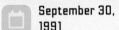

All-Stars
Hall of Fame
21

He's the gold standard for pass protection—he's got muscle and quickness.

After seven seasons and 106 games, David has made his mark. With a grade of 96.8, he won *Pro Football Focus* Pass Blocker of the Year (2018), and was the highest-ranked offensive lineman in 2019. The future for the "Persian Aversion" is looking very shiny—perhaps Lombardi Super Bowl trophy shiny. David is a big guy, but it's his superfast legs that make him the league's top pass protector.

PERSONAL DATA

September 30, 1991

San Mateo, California

6 ft. 4 in.

310 lb.

CAREER HISTORY

GREEN BAY PACKERS

2013 –

★ 69 ★

CAREER HIGHLIGHTS

- Ranked 43rd on the NFL Top 100 (2019).
- Two Pro Bowl and one first team All-Pro selections.
- Two second-team All-Pac–12 selections.

OFFENSIVE TACKLE

TYRON SMITH

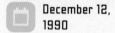

All-Stars
Hall of Fame
24

According to sources, this lineman can bench press 600–700 pounds.

His standout high school track-and-field performance made him a five-star recruit, and on the field that counts, Tyron wins nearly every battle at the line of scrimmage. Even in a down year like 2018, he allowed zero sacks in 15 games. He not only looks like the archetypal offense, he has the technique and athleticism to back it up, especially in the run game. What to watch? Those really long arms!

PERSONAL DATA

📅 December 12, 1990

📍 Los Angeles, California

⬆ 6 ft. 5 in.

⚖ 320 lb.

OFFENSIVE TACKLE

CAREER HISTORY

DALLAS COWBOYS

2011 –

⭐ 77 ⭐

CAREER HIGHLIGHTS

🏈 Seven Pro Bowl and two first team All-Pro selections.

🏈 First team All-Pac–10 and Morris Trophy for top conference lineman (2010).

🏈 Ranked 18th—the highest placed linesman—on NFL Top 100 (2017).

⭐⭐⭐

A. J. GREEN

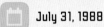

All-Stars
Hall of Fame
26

He's always had reliable hands—at seven he could juggle four items at once.

One of his earliest accolades came in 2008 when *Sports Illustrated* rated him as a number 1 prospect. A.J. is known for his versatility and consistency. He may be chased down, but he eludes capture. He held the NFL record for more passes (260) than any other player in his first three seasons. A.J.'s best catch? Maybe his one-handed touchdown against the Kansas City Chiefs in 2012.

PERSONAL DATA

📅 July 31, 1988

📍 Summerville, South Carolina

⬆ 6 ft. 4 in.

🔒 210 lb.

CAREER HISTORY

CINCINNATI BENGALS

2011 –

★ **18** ★

CAREER HIGHLIGHTS

- Seven Pro Bowl and three second team All-Pro selections.
- Ranked 15th in NFL Top 100 (2016).
- Six seasons with 1,000-plus receiving yards.

WIDE RECEIVER

★ ★ ★

CAM NEWTON

Cam's impressive records and stats are history in the making.

Cam is the only sportsman in the modern era to be the first overall draft pick, win the Heisman Memorial Trophy, and garner a NCAA national championship win in the same year. Four years later, in 2015, he was NFC Offensive Player of the Week five times in just nine weeks—unprecedented! This QB is hard to stop because he's fast, smart, and all muscle. No wonder he's nicknamed "Superman."

PERSONAL DATA

📅 May 11, 1989

📍 Atlanta, Georgia

⬆ 6 ft. 5 in.

⚖ 245 lb.

CAREER HISTORY

CAROLINA PANTHERS

2011 –

⭐ **1** ⭐

CAREER HIGHLIGHTS

🏈 Three Pro Bowl and one first team All-Pro selections.

🏈 First NFL QB to throw for over 400 yards in his first game. He broke the record by 120 yards.

🏈 NFL MVP and Offensive Player of the Year (2015).

QUARTERBACK

LE'VEON BELL

All-Stars Hall of Fame 36

Expect 1,600 scrimmage yards and eight-plus touchdowns a season.

A commentator called Le'Veon "The Great Hesitator" for his patience at the line of scrimmage. A bruising running back, he waits for his blockers to take off before he makes his move. What he may lack in explosive speed, he makes up for in cunning and strategy. He sat out the 2018 season, but his patience paid off with the Jets deal.

PERSONAL DATA

- February 18, 1992
- Reynoldsburg, Ohio
- 6 ft. 1 in.
- 225 lb.

CAREER HISTORY

PITTSBURGH STEELERS
2013 – 2018
★ 26 ★

NEW YORK JETS
2019 –
★ 26 ★

CAREER HIGHLIGHTS

- First team All-American.
- Three Pro Bowl and two first team All-Pro selections.
- Ranked 5th on NFL Top 100 (2018).

RUNNING BACK

MARSHAL YANDA

All-Stars
Hall of Fame
38

Levelheaded and highly respected, he lures opponents to bull-rush him.

Marshal's game prep is meticulous. He watches the next opponent's last six games, taking in every move they might make. He is tough and his technique is finely tuned, allowing very few sacks and rarely making a false move. This guard has solo shoved three defenders out of the way to create a hole. But, after 13 seasons with the Ravens, he announced his retirement. Marshal will be hard to replace.

PERSONAL DATA

 September 15, 1984

 Cedar Rapids, Iowa

6 ft. 4 in.

305 lb.

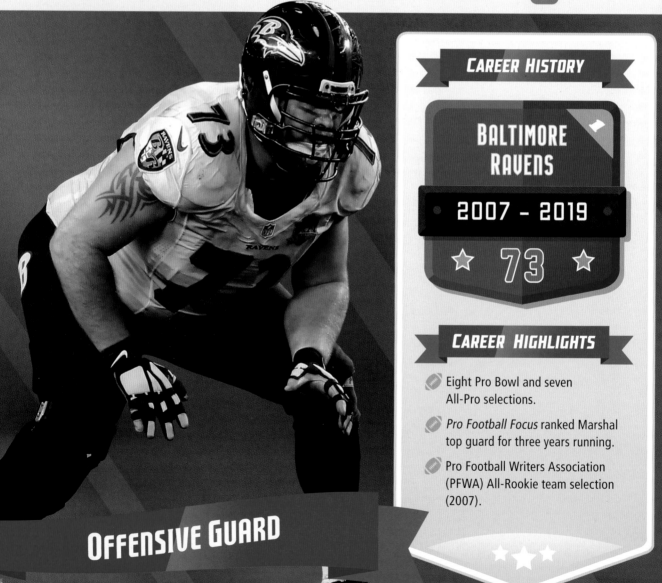

CAREER HISTORY

BALTIMORE RAVENS

2007 - 2019

☆ **73** ☆

CAREER HIGHLIGHTS

🏈 Eight Pro Bowl and seven All-Pro selections.

🏈 *Pro Football Focus* ranked Marshal top guard for three years running.

🏈 Pro Football Writers Association (PFWA) All-Rookie team selection (2007).

OFFENSIVE GUARD

★ ★ ★

RICHARD SHERMAN

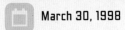

All-Stars
Hall of Fame
40

Called "the best corner in the game" by many—including himself.

This is one cornerback who does not hide his light under a bushel. With the "Legion of Boom," Richard led the Seahawks to the third-largest win margin (43–8) in Super Bowl history. Known for his crafty technique and quick feet, Richard makes big plays. His "Immaculate Deflection" in the NFC Championship against the 49ers is regarded by fans as a franchise highlight.

PERSONAL DATA

March 30, 1998

Compton, California

6 ft. 3 in.

205 lb.

CAREER HISTORY

SEATTLE SEAHAWKS
2011 – 2017
★ 25 ★

SAN FRANCISCO 49ERS
2018 –
☆ 25 ☆

CAREER HIGHLIGHTS

- Five Pro Bowl and three first team All-Pro selections.
- NFC Defensive Player of the Year (2014).
- *Pro Football Focus* Best Cornerback of the Decade.

CORNERBACK

PLAYER POSITIONS

The players used in a game and where they are positioned varies according to the game plan. The information below shows a 4–3 defense and an I–formation offense.

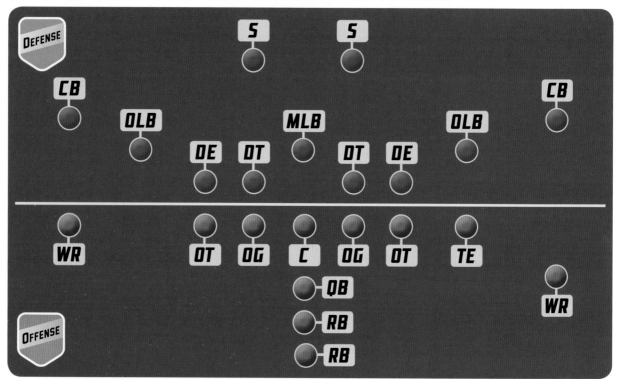

Interior line

C **Center** begins play from the line of scrimmage by snapping the ball to QB.

OG **Offensive guards** block running or passing plays.

OT **Offensive tackles** block running and passing plays.

Backs and receivers

QB **Quarterback** calls the plays, initiates action, and handles the "snap."

RB **Running backs** usually run the ball, but may also catch passes and block.

WR **Wide receivers** are pass–catch specialists who run pass routes and get open for passes.

TE **Tight end** catches passes and blocks.

Defensive line (rushers)

DT **Defensive tackles** rush the passer and stop running plays.

DE **Defensive ends** similar to DTs, but play at edges of defensive line.

Linebackers

LB middle (**MLB**) and outside (**OLB**) linebackers stop RBs, cover pass plays, and rush the QB.

Defensive backs

CB **Cornerbacks** cover wide receivers, break up passes, and tackle players who catch passes.

S **Safeties** assist in pass coverage and make tackles.

GLOSSARY

50,000-yard club QBs who have made 50,000 career passing yards.

ACC Atlantic Coast Conference.

AFC American Football Conference.

All-American select group of college football players.

All-Pac–12 western US collegiate football conference.

All-Pro honor given annually to best player at each position.

ball carrier player who carries the ball on an offensive play.

block when an opposing player obstructs a player's path.

Butkus Award named for Dick Butkus, it honors high school, college, and pro linebackers for athleticism and community work.

combine drills physical tests undertaken by college players.

completions how many QB passes make it to the receiver.

cover when one player stays with an opposing player to prevent catches.

deep-ball pass a throw exceeding more than 20 air yards.

draft annual player selection.

formation which players are positioned on the field and where.

franchise a team authorized by the NFL.

G.O.A.T. greatest of all time.

Heisman Memorial Trophy awarded annually to the top college player for ability, diligence, and perseverance.

huddle when a team comes together to discuss the upcoming play.

Immaculate Deflection (The Tip) a game-saving deflection from Seattle Seahawks' CB to LB in 2013 NFC Championship against the 49ers.

interception when the opposing defense catches the ball from the QB.

Legion of Boom nickname of Seattle Seahawks' defense in the 2010s.

line of scrimmage imaginary line across the field that cannot be crossed until the next play has begun.

Morris Trophy honors top college linemen in Pac–12 (was Pac–10).

MVP Most Valuable Player.

NFC National Football Conference.

NFL Comeback Player of the Year awarded to a player who has overcome hardship or injury.

NFL National Football League consisting of 16 NFC and 16 AFC teams.

NFL Top 100 players with outstanding season performances as voted for by fellow players.

OPOY – NFL Offensive Player of the Year.

pass when the ball is thrown.

pass rush tactic to sack the QB or kicker, or force an error.

passing pocket an area behind the line of scrimmage protected by offensive linemen so QB can pass the ball safely to a receiver.

passing touchdown pass to a receiver that results in a touchdown.

passing yards distance gained by offensive team on completed passes from line of scrimmage to where player was tackled, forced out, or in the end zone.

percentage win/loss/tie how many wins, losses, or tied games a team has had.

Pro Bowl all-star game using players drawn from across the NFL.

Pro Football Hall of Fame the hall of fame for professional football, in Canton, Ohio.

reception catch of a forward pass from behind the line of scrimmage.

receiving touchdowns touchdown scored by a receiver after catching a pass.

receiving yards distance gained by a receiver on a passing play, including ball air yards, and yards after reception.

rookie a player in his NFL first season.

running route path used by a receiver to get into open space for a forward pass.

rush running with the ball from behind the line of scrimmage to gain yards.

sack when the QB is tackled behind the line of scrimmage before he makes a forward pass.

Steve Largent Award presented to Seattle Seahawks players who best represent determination and integrity.

Super Bowl annual championship between NFC and AFC champions. Winner receives the Vince Lombardi Trophy.

tackle physically impede a player (not a QB) with the ball to stop progress.

TFL a tackle behind line of scrimmage carried out by any player other than QB.

touchdown when a team crosses the goal line of the opposition's end zone, resulting in six points.

triple crown a player who tops three statistical categories for his position.

Walter Payton Award annual NFL award honoring a player's volunteer and charity work.

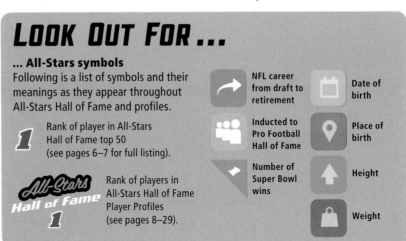

LOOK OUT FOR...

... All-Stars symbols
Following is a list of symbols and their meanings as they appear throughout All-Stars Hall of Fame and profiles.

1 Rank of player in All-Stars Hall of Fame top 50 (see pages 6–7 for full listing).

All-Stars Hall of Fame **1** Rank of players in All-Stars Hall of Fame Player Profiles (see pages 8–29).

NFL career from draft to retirement

Inducted to Pro Football Hall of Fame

Number of Super Bowl wins

Date of birth

Place of birth

Height

Weight

INDEX